Master Class
Model making

Written by Nick Arnold and Vip Patel
Illustrated by Paul Young and Mike Braybrooke

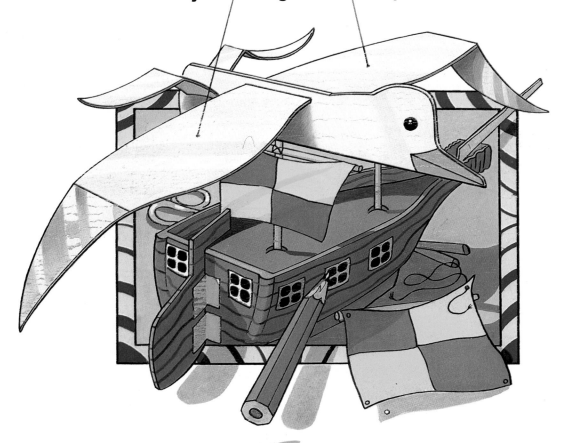

HENDERSON
PUBLISHING PLC

Lovely Bubbly

Your first challenge is simple. Can you blow mega-gigantic bubbles?

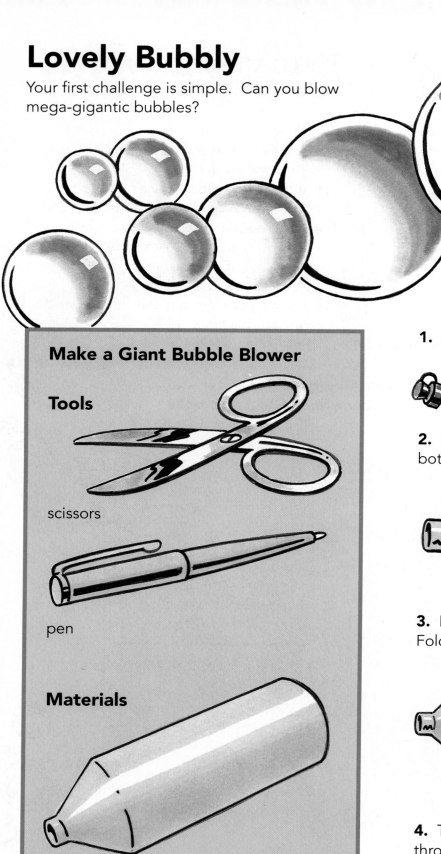

Make a Giant Bubble Blower

Tools

scissors

pen

Materials

clean, empty washing-up liquid bottle

1. Remove the top.

2. Cut the end off the washing-up bottle along line A.

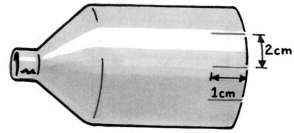

2cm

1cm

3. Draw flaps. Cut them out as shown. Fold down the flaps.

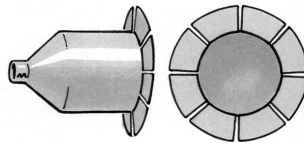

4. To use, dip in the mixture and blow through the top end.

Make a bubble fan

Bubble fans mean extra bubble fun. The second part of this challenge is to blow different sized bubbles at the same time.

Why bubbles float

A bubble is an air pocket with a stretchy detergent and water skin. Bubbles float because they are lighter (less dense) than water.

Why bubbles fly

Bubbles float in the air because they are mostly air themselves. Although bubbles are a little heavier than air, they are so light that any air movement will lift them upwards. Try blowing gently or making a breeze with your bubble fan. Do you think big bubbles fly as high as little bubbles? Check by using your fan to make different sized bubbles.

Sticky Bubble Mixture

Sugar is the secret ingredient which makes the bubbles last longer.

Ingredients
washing-up liquid
water
sugar

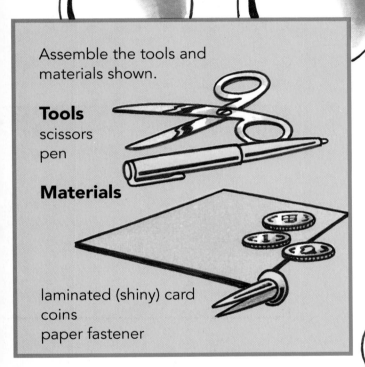

Assemble the tools and materials shown.

Tools
scissors
pen

Materials
laminated (shiny) card
coins
paper fastener

Directions

Fill a bowl half full of warm water and stir in washing-up liquid until the mixture is really bubbly. Add 3 tablespoonfuls of white sugar.

3. Repeat steps 2 and 3 to make two more shapes.

4. Ask an adult to help you make a hole in the base of the shapes as shown. Secure the segments with a paper fastener.

5. To use, stir in the bubble mixture. Open the fan and blow!

1. Draw a shape on the card as shown. Draw around some coins to make circles of different sizes.

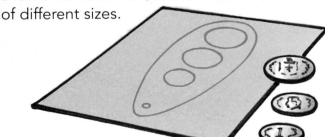

2. Cut out the circles. Cut out the card shape.

Part One:
FLOATING

All About Boats

Now see if you can make a boat that floats! Assemble the tools and materials shown.

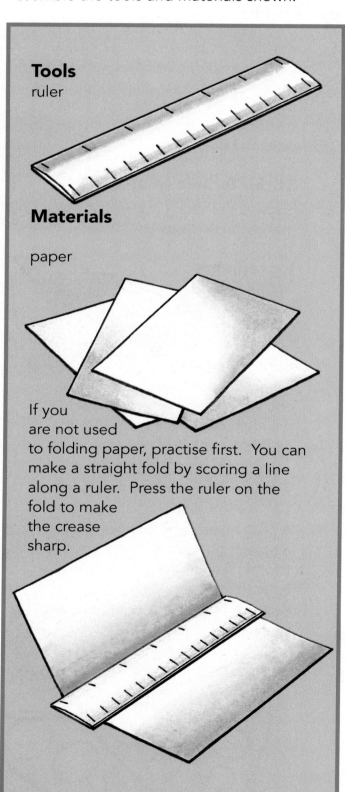

Tools
ruler

Materials

paper

If you are not used to folding paper, practise first. You can make a straight fold by scoring a line along a ruler. Press the ruler on the fold to make the crease sharp.

1. Fold the paper in half lengthwise as shown.

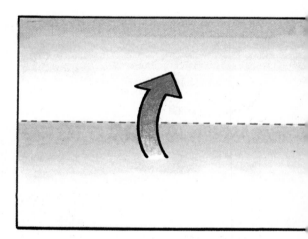

2. Turn the corners up to the size shown.

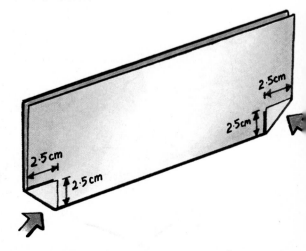

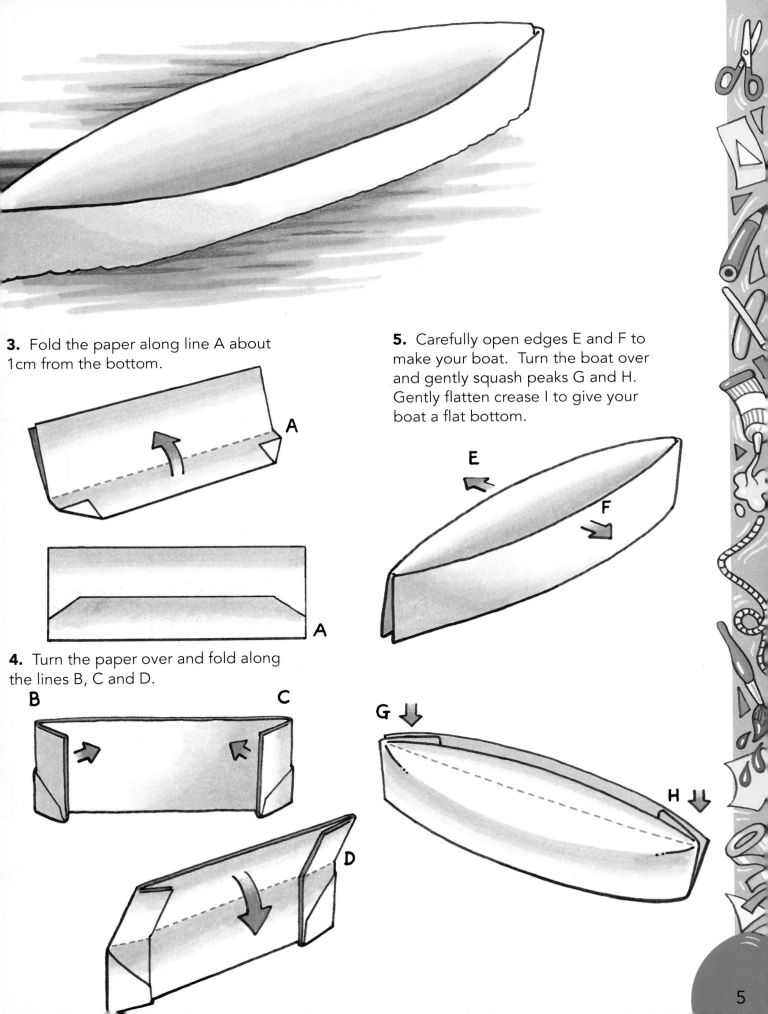

3. Fold the paper along line A about 1cm from the bottom.

A

A

4. Turn the paper over and fold along the lines B, C and D.

B   C

D

5. Carefully open edges E and F to make your boat. Turn the boat over and gently squash peaks G and H. Gently flatten crease I to give your boat a flat bottom.

E

F

G ⬇

H ⬇⬇

5

Sea Trials

After a ship is built it does not go into service straight away. It undergoes sea trials to check that it will sail safely. The second part of this challenge is to sail your boat fully laden.

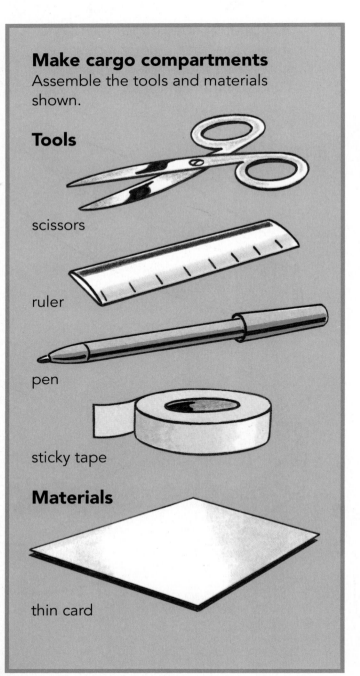

Make cargo compartments
Assemble the tools and materials shown.

Tools

scissors

ruler

pen

sticky tape

Materials

thin card

1. Carefully measure the length and depth of your boat.

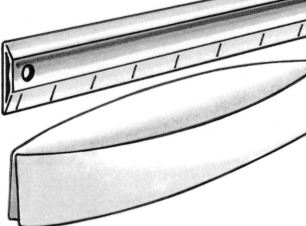

2. Cut a piece of card to size. Cut two slots to half the depth of the card.

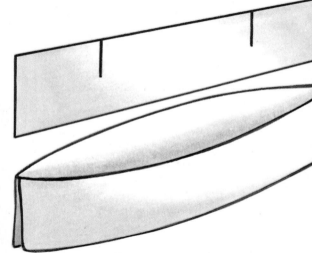

Get together some coins, marbles, dried peas or other small heavy items. Place your boat in some water and discover the effect of putting weight in some compartments and not in others. Can you see why it's important for a cargo to be evenly distributed?

3. Place the card lengthwise in the boat and measure the width of the boat at the slots.

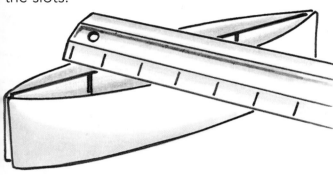

4. Cut semi-circles of card to fit the width and depth of the boat at the slots. Cut slots from the bottom of the semi-circles as shown.

How it Works
Even heavy ships can float because they contain air in their holds and cabins. This makes them lighter than the same volume of water. But if one part of the ship is heavier, the ship will be lower in the water at that point and will not float evenly.

5. Assemble the pieces of card as shown to make bulkheads. You can use sticky tape to strengthen the bulkheads. Place the completed bulkheads in the boat.

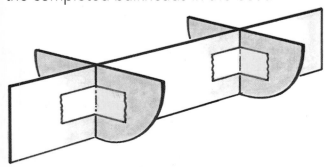

Investigating Floating

Over 2,000 years ago, a Greek scientist called Archimedes noticed that the water level rose when he got in the bath. "Eureka!" he cried. He had discovered displacement. This means that whatever you put in water will always push out, or displace, its own weight in water.

Can you devise a Plimsoll line measurer? Assemble the tools and materials shown.

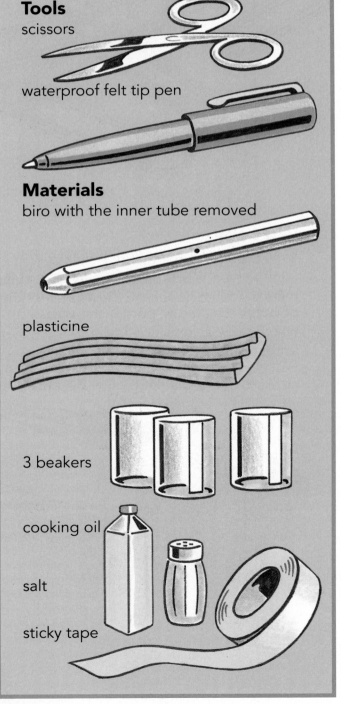

Tools
scissors

waterproof felt tip pen

Materials
biro with the inner tube removed

plasticine

3 beakers

cooking oil

salt

sticky tape

FLOATING FACT
The Dead Sea in Israel is so salty that people can float about in it effortlessly!

The weight of water can vary. Salt water is heavier than fresh water because of the extra salt it contains. Cold water is heavier than warm water. This means that a ship in a cold sea displaces less water than it would in warm fresh water. Ships have a plimsoll line to predict safe loading levels in different kinds of water.

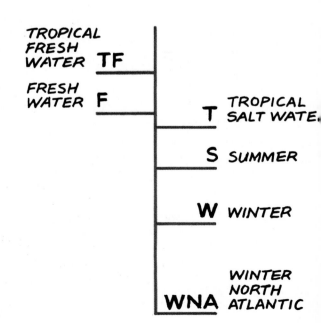

TROPICAL FRESH WATER **TF**

FRESH WATER **F**

T TROPICAL SALT WATER

S SUMMER

W WINTER

WNA WINTER NORTH ATLANTIC

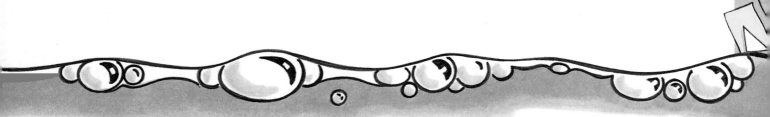

Directions

1. If your biro has a hole in the side, cover it with sticky tape. Stick a blob of plasticine on the bottom end of the biro.

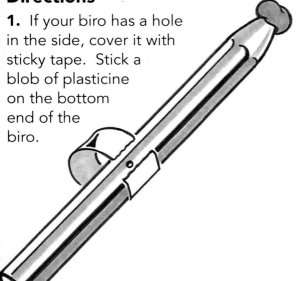

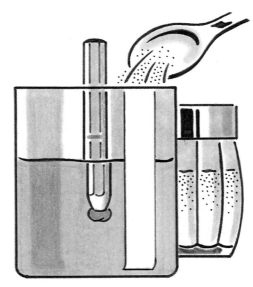

3. Dissolve three tablespoonfuls of salt in another beaker. Float your measurer and mark the water level. You will see that the measurer floats higher in the salty water.

4. Now try the measurer in a beaker of cooking oil. It will float lower because the oil is lighter than water.

2. Fill a beaker with water and float the biro upright in it. Mark the water level on the side of the biro.

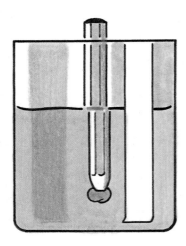

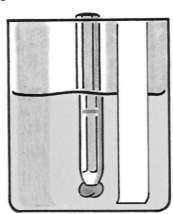

Water Crawlers

Some creatures are so light, they can live on the surface of the water. This pond skater spreads its long legs to walk on the surface without breaking the water tension. Water tension is caused by the attraction of tiny water molecules. They ensure that the surface is pulled downwards to make a tight skin.

For this challenge you have to make your own water crawler.

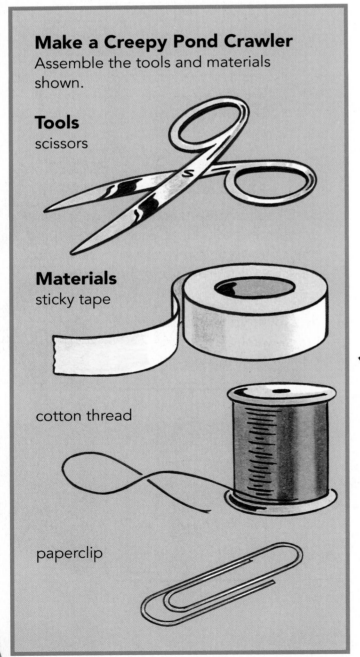

Make a Creepy Pond Crawler
Assemble the tools and materials shown.

Tools
scissors

Materials
sticky tape

cotton thread

paperclip

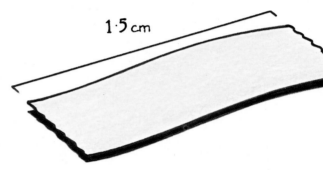

1. Cut a piece of tape 1.5cm long and place it face up.

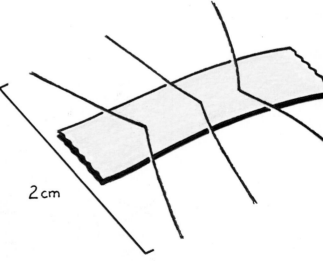

2. Cut three lengths of thread each 2cm long. Carefully stick the thread to the tape as shown.

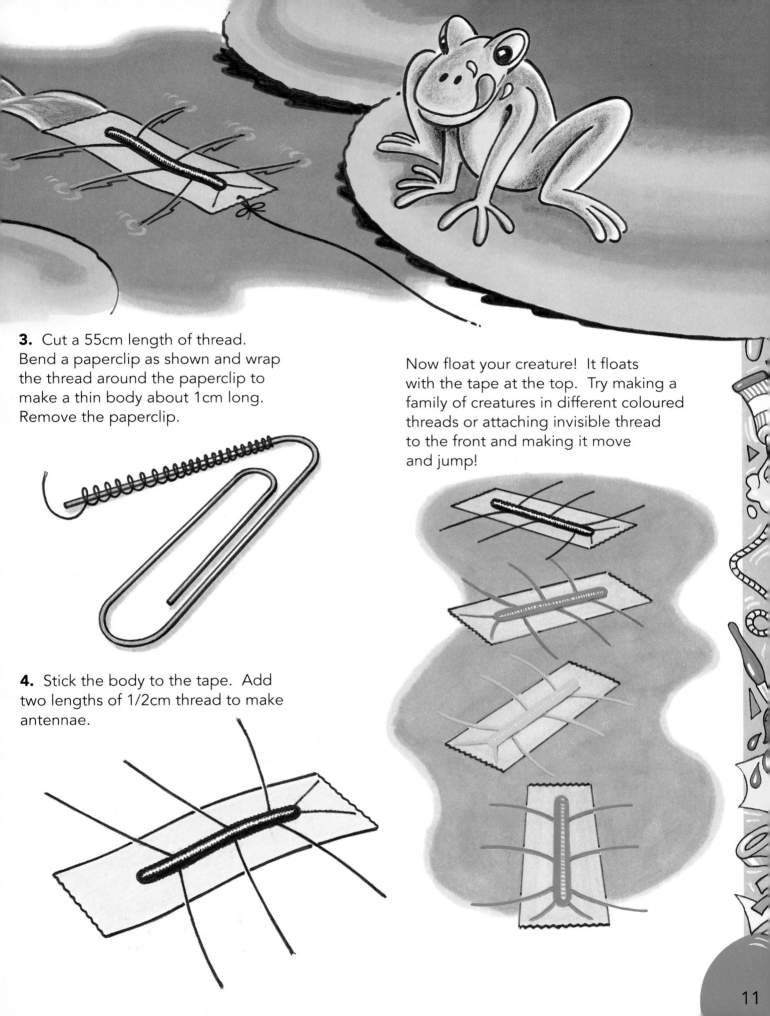

3. Cut a 55cm length of thread. Bend a paperclip as shown and wrap the thread around the paperclip to make a thin body about 1cm long. Remove the paperclip.

4. Stick the body to the tape. Add two lengths of 1/2cm thread to make antennae.

Now float your creature! It floats with the tape at the top. Try making a family of creatures in different coloured threads or attaching invisible thread to the front and making it move and jump!

A Speedy Boat

Here is a second water tension challenge. Try making this boat which uses the power of surface tension to move through the water.

Assemble the tools and materials shown.

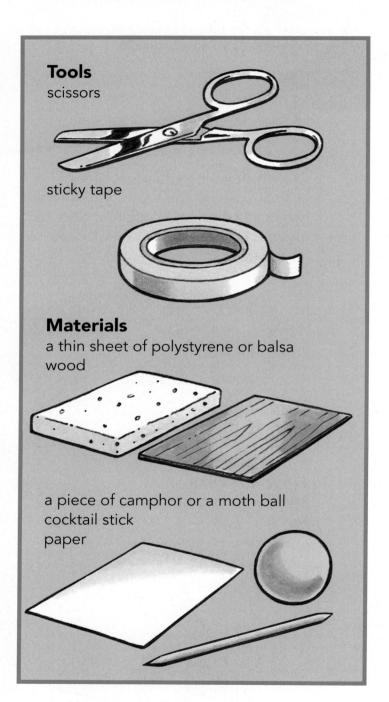

Tools
scissors

sticky tape

Materials
a thin sheet of polystyrene or balsa wood

a piece of camphor or a moth ball
cocktail stick
paper

Instructions

1. Cut the polystyrene or balsa wood into the size shown.

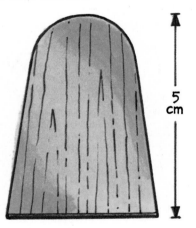

5 cm

2. Ask an adult to help you cut the polystyrene or balsa wood into the boat shape shown.

3. Turn the boat over and cover the bottom of the rear notch with a loop of parcel tape as shown.

4. Make the mast and sail out of a cocktail stick and a triangle of paper. Secure the sail to the mast with sticky tape. Stick the cocktail stick into the polystyrene boat. If you are using balsa wood, use a tiny blob of plasticine to make the mast stand upright.

Testing

1. Place the moth ball in the rear notch on the parcel tape. Watch it push the boat along.

How it works

The camphor destroys the surface tension behind the boat. This makes the surface tension in front of the boat pull the craft forward.

13

Underwater Bells

Things sink because they are heavier (denser) than the water they displace. In this challenge you have to make your own diving bell.

Make a Diving Bell

Assemble the tools and materials shown.

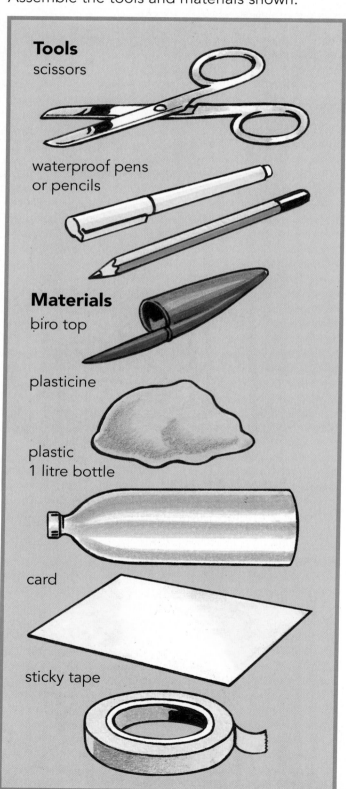

Tools
scissors

waterproof pens
or pencils

Materials
biro top

plasticine

plastic
1 litre bottle

card

sticky tape

Instructions

1. Fill the bottle with water almost to the top.

2. Make sure the biro top is one with a closed end. Roll a piece of plasticine about 3cm long and push it into the base of the biro top as shown.

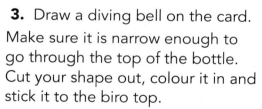

3. Draw a diving bell on the card. Make sure it is narrow enough to go through the top of the bottle. Cut your shape out, colour it in and stick it to the biro top.

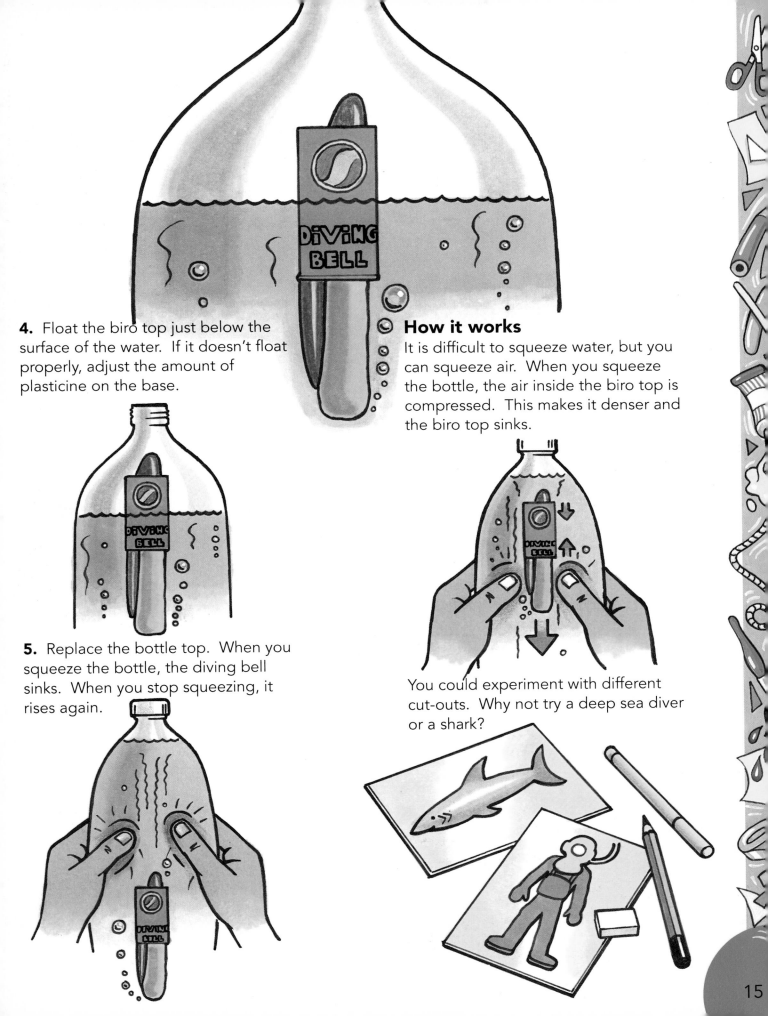

4. Float the biro top just below the surface of the water. If it doesn't float properly, adjust the amount of plasticine on the base.

5. Replace the bottle top. When you squeeze the bottle, the diving bell sinks. When you stop squeezing, it rises again.

How it works

It is difficult to squeeze water, but you can squeeze air. When you squeeze the bottle, the air inside the biro top is compressed. This makes it denser and the biro top sinks.

You could experiment with different cut-outs. Why not try a deep sea diver or a shark?

That Sinking Feeling

Have you ever wanted to live in a submarine?
In this challenge you can try the next best thing.

Assemble the tools and materials shown.

Tools
scissors

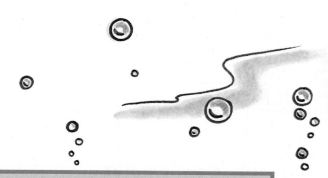

waterproof
felt-tip
pens
ruler

Materials

1 litre plastic
bottle

balloon
parcel tape
coins or other small metal weights.
5 long plastic straws
3 small rubber bands
wipe-clean match box wrapper

Instructions
1. Make holes in the sides and top of the bottle as shown. Make the top hole the same size as the end of the match box wrapper. Use parcel tape to secure the weights to the side of the bottle as shown.

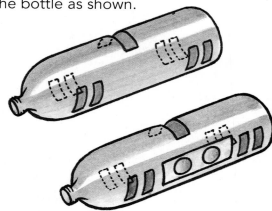

2. Wrap parcel tape around the match box wrapper. Use two rubber bands to bind the straws together. Insert the straws through the wrapper as shown.

3. Insert the ends of the straws through the neck of the balloon and secure tightly with a rubber band. Wrap parcel tape to secure the join between the balloon and the straws.

4. Pass the balloon through the hole as shown. Slot the match box wrapper into the hole. Cover the join with parcel tape.

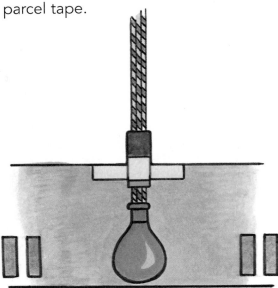

5. Cover the bottle with parcel tape. Use the pens to draw portholes and insignia on the sides. Do not cover up the holes in the sides.

Your submarine is now ready for testing! Place it carefully in the bath. Allow it to sink. Then blow through the straws and watch it surface.

How it works

Real submarines can also take air from the surface though tubes. Like a proper submarine, your model takes in water when it sinks and expels water when it rises. A real submarine uses special ballast tanks and pumps to do this.

Make a Treasure Galleon!

Long before there were submarines, wooden sailing ships ruled the waves. You've seen them in films, in this ambitious challenge you get the chance to make your own!

Making the hull

The main body of a ship is called the hull. Assemble the tools and materials shown.

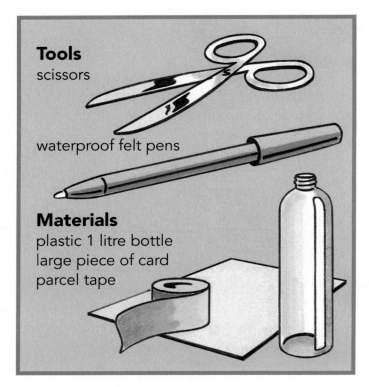

Tools
scissors

waterproof felt pens

Materials
plastic 1 litre bottle
large piece of card
parcel tape

Instructions

1. Ask an adult to cut the bottle in half lengthwise. They should wear gardening gloves and begin by cutting the rim downwards using a serrated knife. They should next place the bottle on its side and continue cutting using strong kitchen scissors.

2. Cover the outside of one of the halves with parcel tape and use waterproof pens to draw a pattern of planks, gun ports and stern windows.

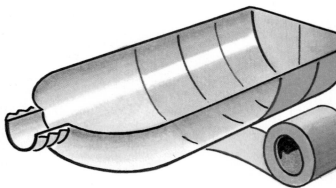

3. Place the half bottle on the card and draw around it. Cut out the shape you have drawn. Draw a pattern of planks and hatches on the card. Make holes in the card for the masts.

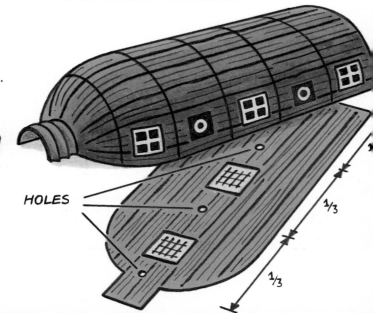

HOLES

1/3

1/3

1/3

Making the Keel

Assemble the tools and materials shown.

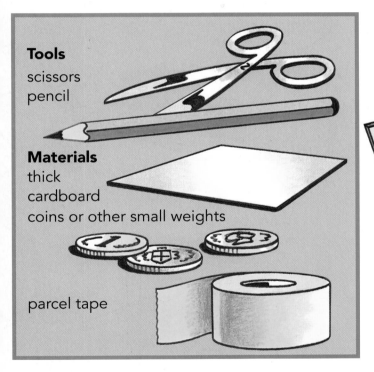

Tools
scissors
pencil

Materials
thick
cardboard
coins or other small weights

parcel tape

Instructions

1. Cut out the keel shape as shown. Then draw around it on the remaining cardboard to make a second shape.

2. Use parcel tape to secure the coins to one of the shapes and bind the shapes together with more tape.

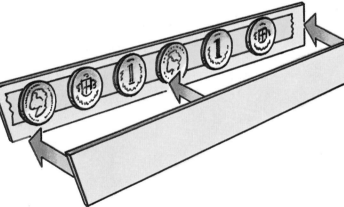

3. Use more parcel tape to secure the keel to the base of the hull.

Galleon - continued

Making the Masts and Rudder
Assemble the tools and materials shown.

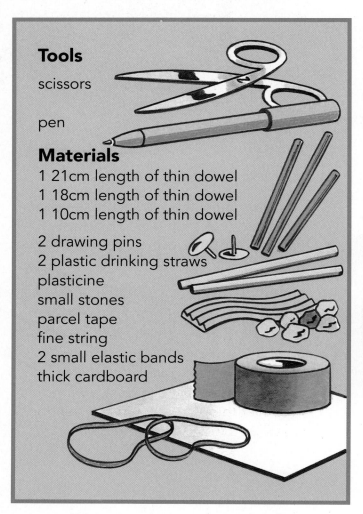

Tools
scissors

pen

Materials
1 21cm length of thin dowel
1 18cm length of thin dowel
1 10cm length of thin dowel

2 drawing pins
2 plastic drinking straws
plasticine
small stones
parcel tape
fine string
2 small elastic bands
thick cardboard

Instructions
1. If necessary, ask an adult to cut the lengths of dowel to size. Push them through the mast holes in the deck.

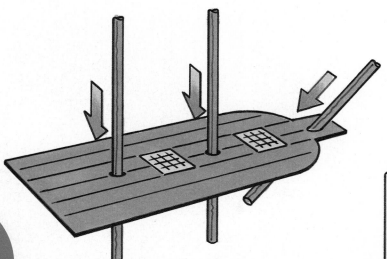

2. Fit the deck to the hull as shown. Secure the edge with more parcel tape. Before the deck is finally in place, use plasticine to secure the end of the dowels to the base of the hull as shown. Arrange a few stones in the base of the hull as ballast.

3. Cut 10cm length of straws and attach them to each mast with a drawing pin. Secure the joins with the small elastic bands.

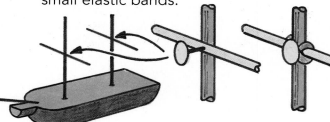

4. To make the rudder, measure the depth at the back of the hull. Draw and cut out a rudder shape in thick cardboard. Use small strips of parcel tape to secure the rudder as shown.

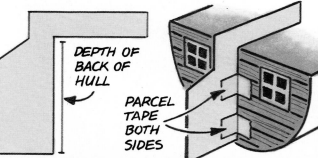

DEPTH OF BACK OF HULL

PARCEL TAPE BOTH SIDES

Making the sails

1. Assemble the tools and materials shown.

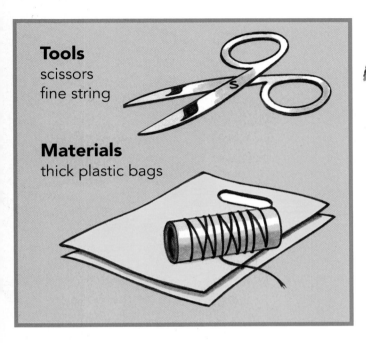

Tools
scissors
fine string

Materials
thick plastic bags

Instructions

1. Cut out two sails from the plastic bags. The sails should be 10cm square.

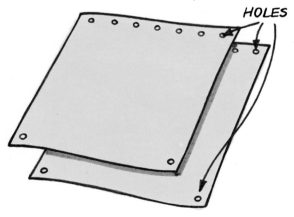

HOLES

2. Use short lengths of string to tie the sails in place as shown.

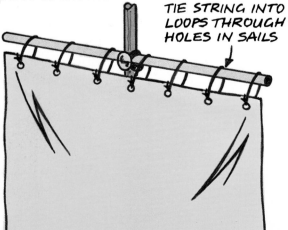

TIE STRING INTO LOOPS THROUGH HOLES IN SAILS

3. Add the rigging and a paper flag of your own design as shown.

Testing the galleon

Your galleon is only suitable for the bath. Try blowing on the sails through cardboard tubes. Practise turning the rudder from side to side. See how the galleon copes with gentle waves. If you let the plug out you can see how it sails in a whirlpool!

Full Steam Ahead!

The age of sail ended with the invention of the steam driven paddle steamers. This next challenge is a bit like the galleon, but it has paddles as well.

Note: Before you make this model, read the instructions on pages 18 - 20 to make the hull, keel and rudder of the galleon and assemble the tools and materials shown on those pages.

Instructions

1. Follow instructions 1 - 3 on page 18 for making the galleon hull.

2. Follow instructions 1 - 3 on page 19 for making the keel of the galleon.

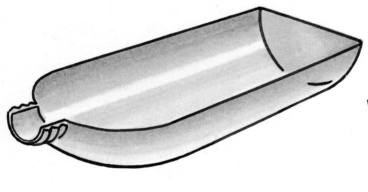

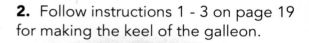

3. Follow instruction 4 on page 20 for making the rudder.

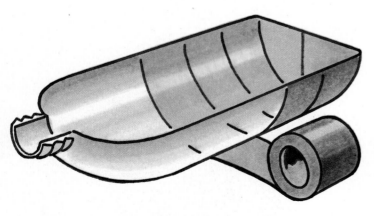

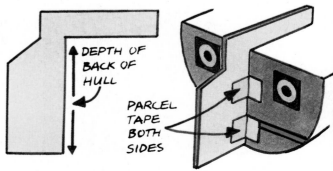

DEPTH OF BACK OF HULL

PARCEL TAPE BOTH SIDES

Paddle Power

3. Cut eight rectangles of card, each 5 x 2cm. Use parcel tape to secure four card rectangles to the cotton reel as shown. Repeat for other cotton reel.

4. Push the pencil through the slots in the hull sides.

5. Thread the beads or plastic washers through the pencil ends on either side of the hull. Thread the cotton reels through the pencil ends. Secure with drawing pins pressed into the pencil ends.

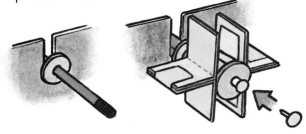

6. Secure the top of the slots with parcel tape.

Testing

1. Before you test your paddle steamer, add a little cooking oil between the bead or washer and the hull. This helps the wheels go around faster. Notice how the wheels go around as you push the craft through the water. In real life a steam engine would supply the power.

Tools

pen
scissors

Materials

2 cotton reels
laminated card
parcel tape
plasticine
bead or plastic washer with a hole large enough for a pencil
pencil thin enough for cotton reels to spin on

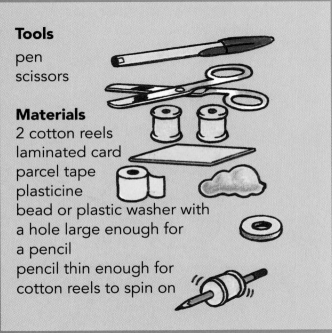

Instructions

1. Ask an adult to cut the pencil to 17cm long.

2. Cut a slot in the middle of each side of the hull. Each slot should be 2cm deep and 7mm wide.

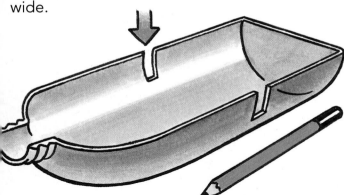

Make a Jet Ski

Have you ever seen a jet ski? In this challenge you can make your own! Assemble the tools and materials shown.

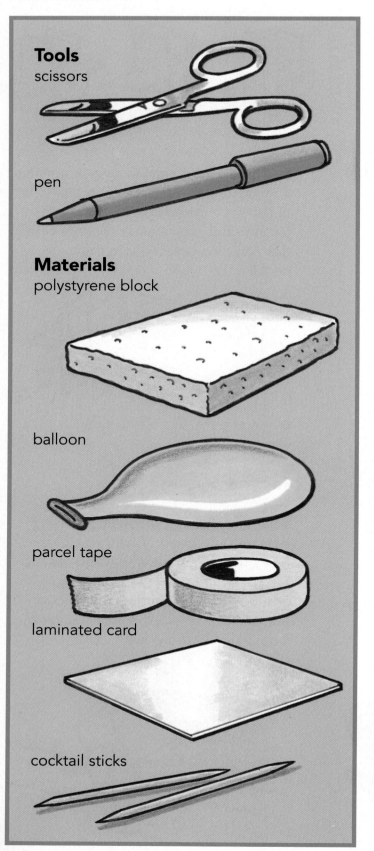

Tools
scissors

pen

Materials
polystyrene block

balloon

parcel tape

laminated card

cocktail sticks

Instructions
1. Fill the balloon with water and knot the end. Attach it underneath the polystyrene block with parcel tape.

2. Cut out the handlebar shape in card and use small pieces of parcel tape to attach it to the cocktail stick as shown. Stick the handlebar assembly in the top of the polystyrene block.

Testing

Place the model in the bath so that the balloon is under the water. Use a pin to make a small hole in the balloon and then widen the hole if necessary using scissors. To use the model again, simply replace the balloon. In real life, the hydroplanes would act like underwater wings and help to lift the craft.

3. To make the hydroplanes, cut out two pieces of card 7 x 2cm. Stick a half a cocktail stick to each piece of card with parcel tape. Push the other ends of the sticks at an upwards angle into the sides of the polystyrene block. Bend the hydroplanes slightly as shown.

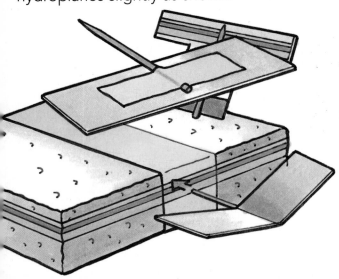

Part Two:
FLYING

Is it a bird - is it a plane?
The second part of this book is about flying.
The first challenge is one of the easiest.
All you need is a piece of A4 paper.

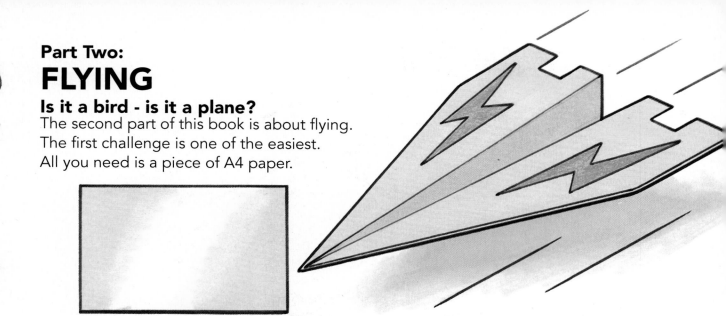

1. Fold the paper in half lengthwise and draw lines as shown. Add lettering or logos in the places shown.

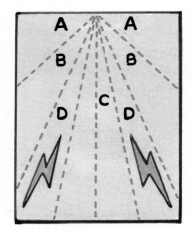

2. Turn the paper over so that your lines face downwards. Turn the corners back to line A and fold. Repeat for lines B.

3. Fold along the centre line C so that the wing lettering is facing inwards and the logos face outwards. Fold the wings downwards at line D.

Testing
Throw strongly and slightly upwards. To hold the dart together try adding a paperclip at crease C. Note how the position of the paperclip affects the flight. Cut slots E and F in each wing. Fold the flaps up to make the plane rise and down to make it sink.

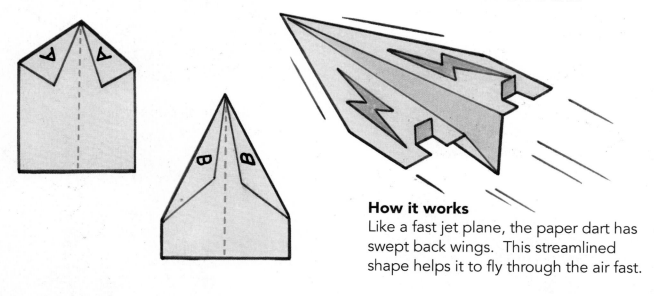

How it works
Like a fast jet plane, the paper dart has swept back wings. This streamlined shape helps it to fly through the air fast.

Make an aerofoil flier

The second part of this challenge shows you how planes stay airborne. Their aerofoil shaped wings provide lift in the air.

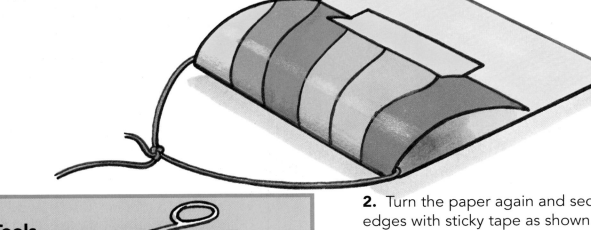

Tools
scissors
coloured
pens or
pencils

Materials

paper

sticky tape

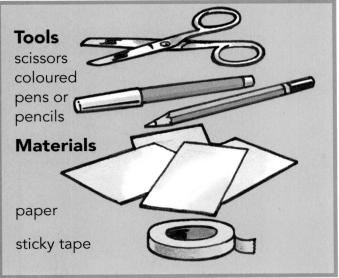

Instructions

1. Cut the paper to size and fold it along line A. Turn the paper over and decorate it.

16·5 cm

cm

7·5 cm   9 cm

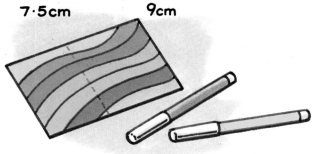

2. Turn the paper again and secure the edges with sticky tape as shown. Make sure that the lower surface is flat and upper surface is curved.

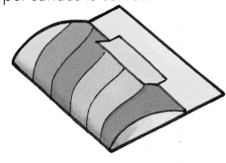

3. Loop and knot some thread as shown.

Try running, pulling the aerofoil behind you.

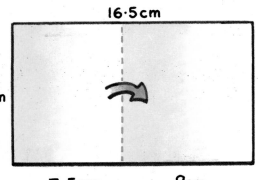

Investigating Flying

Here's a natural challenge. How many different birds have you seen? Most birds are good fliers but not all birds fly in the same way. Small birds flap from tree to tree, large birds may glide or soar high in the sky.

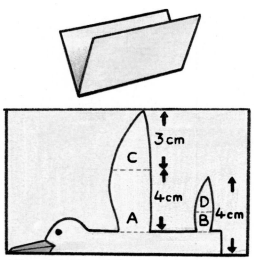

Tools
pen

scissors

Materials

thick paper

sticky tape

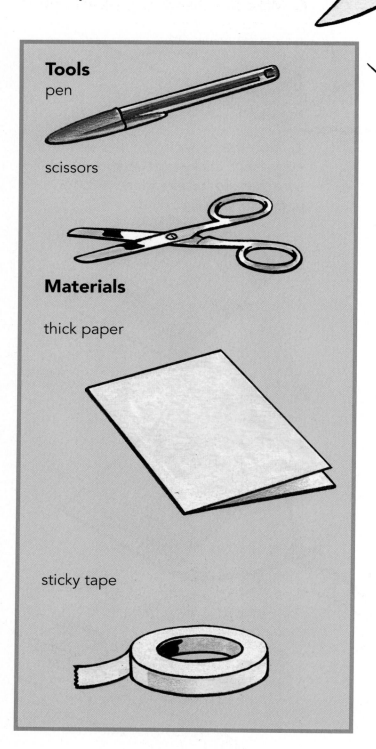

Instructions

1. Fold the paper in half. Draw a bird shape on one side as shown.

2. Cut the shape out. Draw in the bird details on either side of the card. Fold down the wings at lines A and the tail at lines B.

Bird wings are aerofoil shaped to provide lift. The long flight feathers are closed when the wing beats downward and open during the up-stroke.

Gliding and Soaring

Once in the air, birds with a large wingspan can glide on the wind without having to beat their wings. When the bird wants to go higher it spirals up a thermal. Thermals are columns of rising hot air. They are found where the ground has become especially warm.

4. Make sure the wings are level and are in the position shown.

3. Bend the wings down slightly at line C and the tail tips up at line D. Join the two halves of the head and the back behind the wings with sticky tape as shown.

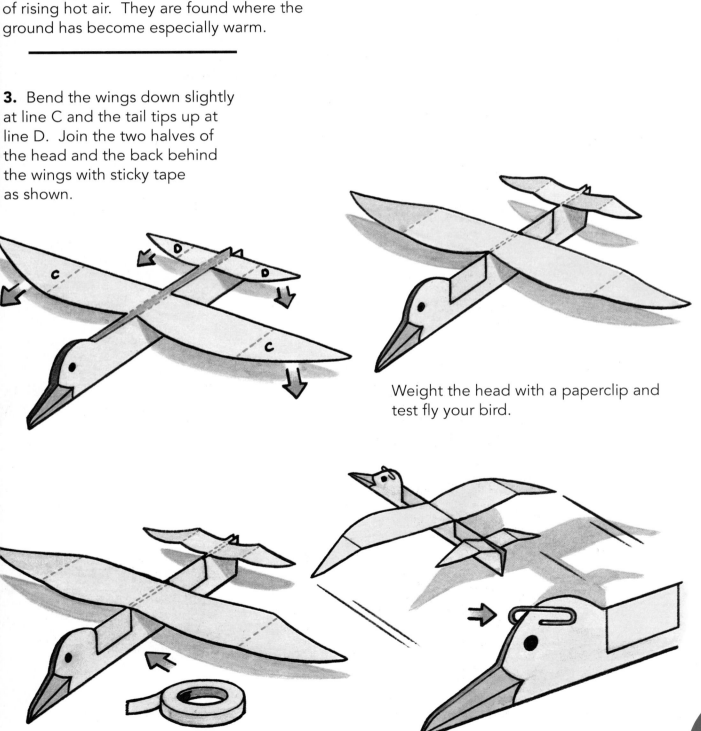

Weight the head with a paperclip and test fly your bird.

29

Scary Bat Flier

For this next challenge you mustn't be scared of bats!

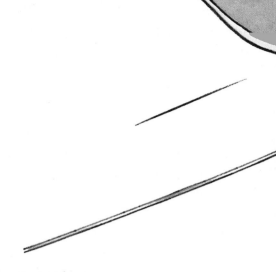

FLYING FACT

When bats hunt they let out high pitched noises and use the echoes to find their prey. Their wings are formed from skin stretched between their long finger bones.

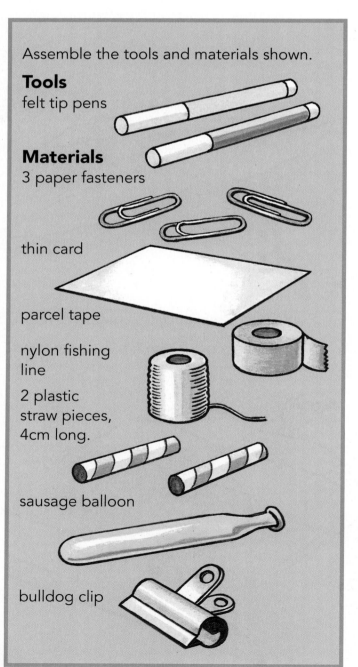

Assemble the tools and materials shown.

Tools
felt tip pens

Materials
3 paper fasteners

thin card

parcel tape

nylon fishing line

2 plastic straw pieces, 4cm long.

sausage balloon

bulldog clip

Instructions

1. Look at some pictures of bats. Try drawing them to get an idea of how they look.

2. Draw and cut some bat wings from stiff card as shown.

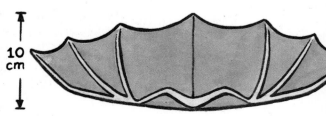

10 cm

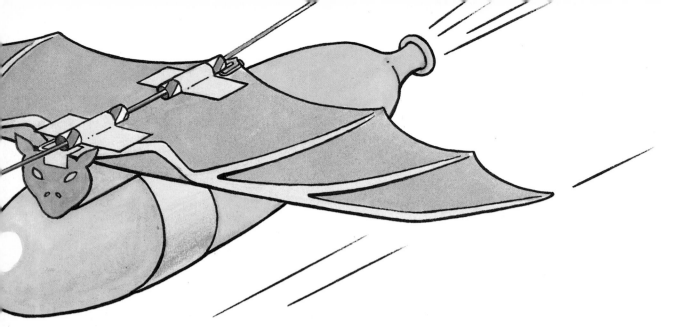

3. Make the body from a toilet roll tube with a paper mask taped to the front as shown. Use the paper fasteners to attach the wings to the body.

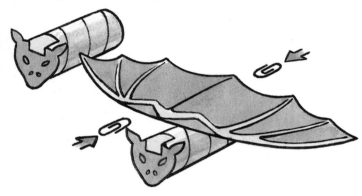

4. Tape the plastic straw lengths to the top of the centre of the wings.

5. Inflate and tape a long balloon to the underside of the body. Secure the inflated balloon with a bulldog clip.

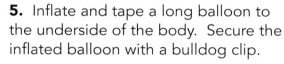
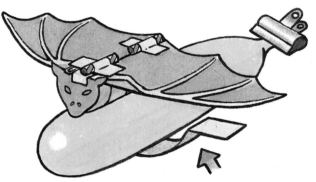

Stretch some fishing line between two trees outdoors or between chairs in a big room. Before you tie the second knot, thread the line through the drinking straw. Take the bat to the end of the line and release the bulldog clip.

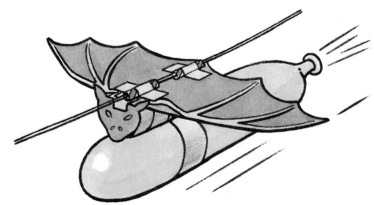

Safety Note
It's fun to fly your bat at twilight but make sure there is no-one in the way.

Flying High

This ambitious challenge is for high fliers! Assemble the tools and materials shown.

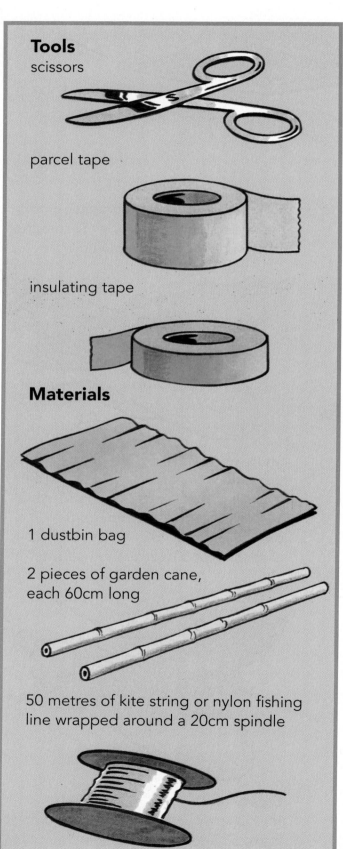

Tools
scissors

parcel tape

insulating tape

Materials

1 dustbin bag

2 pieces of garden cane, each 60cm long

50 metres of kite string or nylon fishing line wrapped around a 20cm spindle

Instructions
1. Lay the dustbin bag flat and cut out the shape shown.

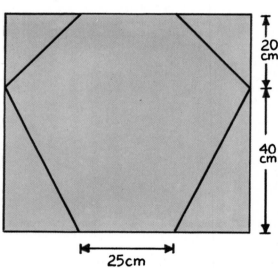

20 cm

40 cm

25cm

2. Cut 2 small triangular vents as shown. These allow air through and keep the kite level.

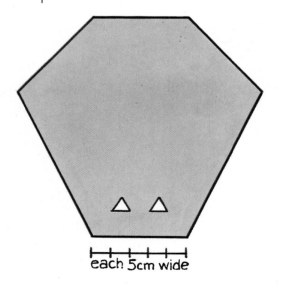

each 5cm wide

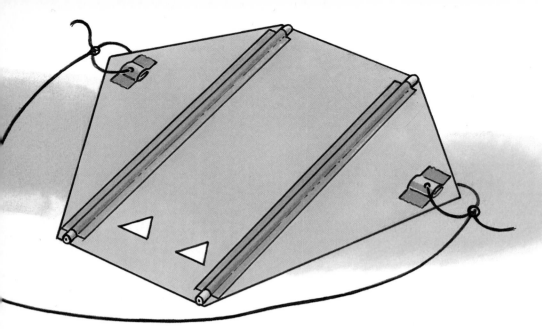

3. Place the canes in the position shown and attach them to the kite with parcel tape.

5. Cut a 3 metre length of kite line. Loop one end through a hole and knot it tightly. Loop and knot the middle of the line. Loop and knot the other end through the other hole.

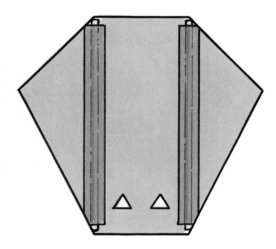

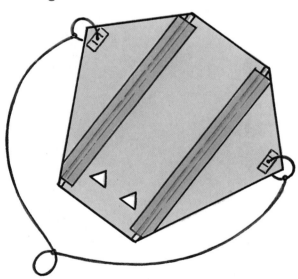

4. Use insulating tape to make a lozenge shape on either side of the kite. Make a small hole in the centre.

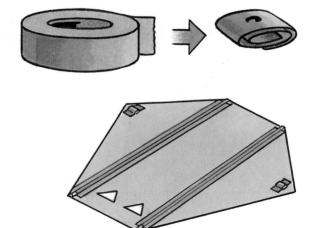

6. Loop and knot the end of the kite line to the middle loop.

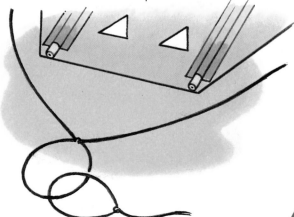

Kite - continued

Flying instructions

> ### Safety note
> Always fly your kite in an open space away from trees, railways, airports, roads or power cables. Never fly a kite in a storm.

1. Ask a friend to stand a good distance downwind and hold the kite up as far as they can.

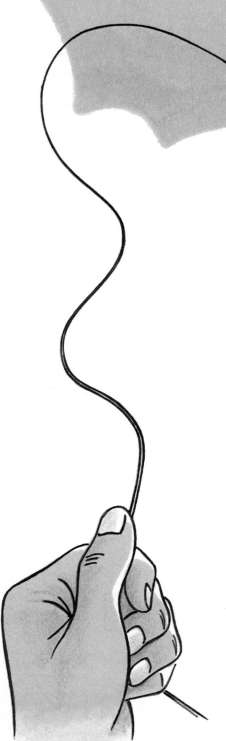

2. They should release the kite as it begins to rise. Gently tug on the string to make the kite climb.

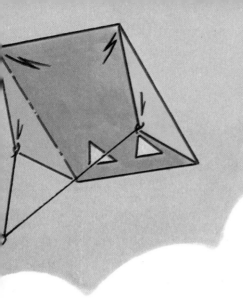

FLYING FACT
People were flying kites in China and Japan thousands of years ago. Japanese "Nagasaki" kites sometimes have lines coated with a glue and powdered glass mixture. Kite flying contestants use their sharp lines to cut each others' kites free!

3. Avoid strong winds. Make sure you carry some scissors, string and spare tape to make emergency repairs.

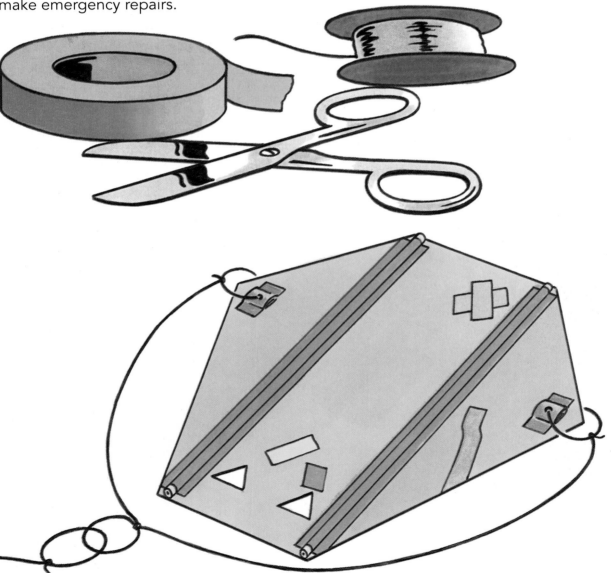

Up, up and away!

The first balloon took off in 1787. It was made of linen paper by the Montgolfier brothers of Lyon, France. In this easy challenge you can go for a balloon flight without leaving the ground! Assemble the tools and materials shown.

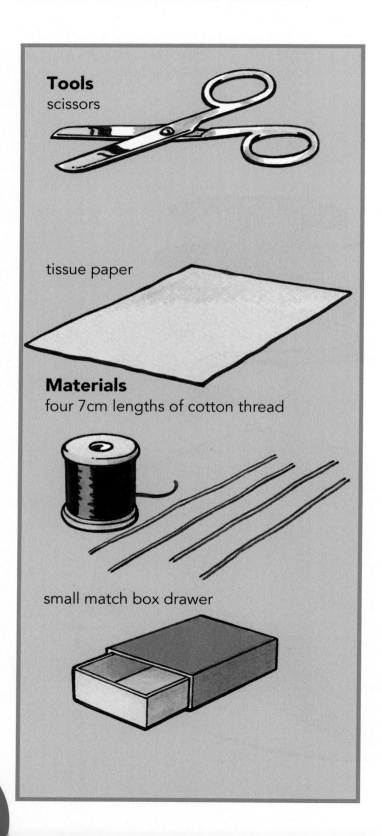

Tools
scissors

tissue paper

Materials
four 7cm lengths of cotton thread

small match box drawer

Instructions

1. Cut out a piece of tissue paper as shown.

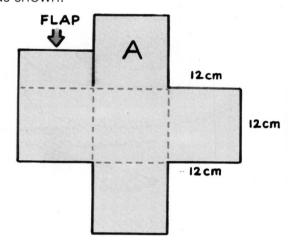

FLAP

A

12 cm

12 cm

12 cm

2. Fold the tissue paper pieces to make an open ended box shape. Secure the flap over side A with sticky tape. Cover the lower edges of the box with sticky tape.

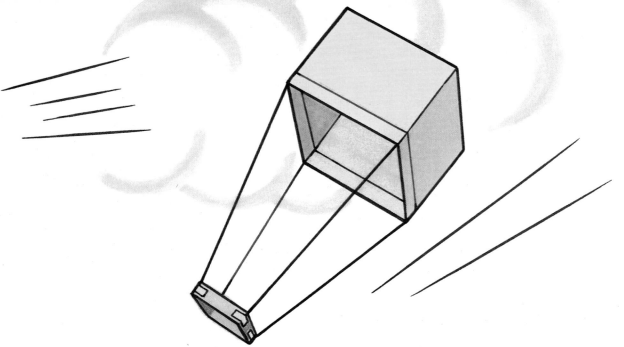

3. Make holes in each lower corner of the box. Knot a length of thread in each of the corner holes.

4. Use sticky tape to attach the ends of the threads to the corners of the matchbox drawer.

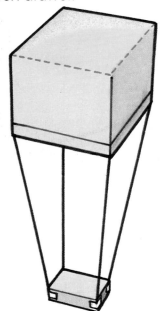

Flying instructions

The balloon rises up when the canopy fills with hot air. Ask an adult to help you use the hair dryer.

Safety note

Keep the hair dryer on a medium setting and well away from the tissue paper.

You could make tiny paper figures and put them in the matchbox drawer as passengers.

Bale Out!

A parachute is a little like a balloon. They are both made of light materials and trap air under fabric. But a parachute is designed to fall rather than rise. If you are going up in a balloon you should also take up this parachute challenge.

Assemble the tools and materials shown.

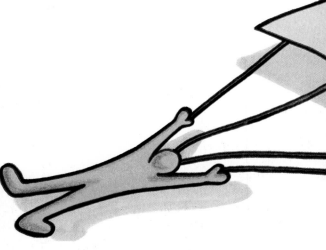

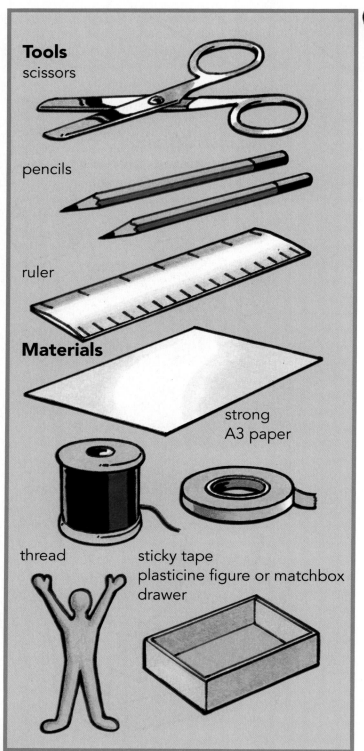

Tools
scissors

pencils

ruler

Materials

strong
A3 paper

thread

sticky tape
plasticine figure or matchbox
drawer

Instructions

1. Cut four 35cm pieces of thread

2. Use sticky tape to secure the thread to the corners of the paper as shown.

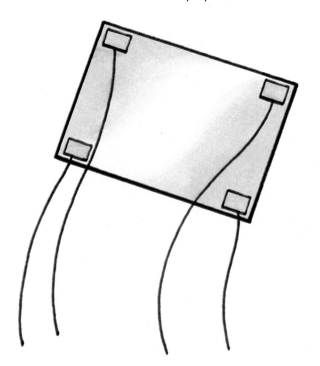

3. Tie the free ends of the threads to a small plasticine person or plasticine weighted matchbox drawer.

Testing it
Stand on a table and drop your parachute. You may need to alter the size of your plasticine person or weight in order to get your parachute to work properly.

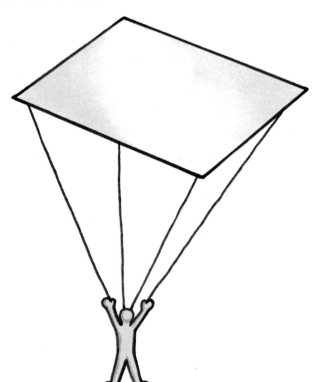

How It Works
A parachute has a large surface area. Some parachutes are 30 metres square. As the parachute falls, it pushes against the air causing air resistance which slows the descent. The weight of the person keeps the parachute open and the parachute can be steered using the cords.

Go with a Whizz

Helicopters differ from ordinary planes in that their 'wings' go around. This allows the helicopter to take off vertically and hover in one place. Like plane wings, helicopter blades are aerofoil shaped to lift the machine in the air. Can you make this helicopter whizzer?

Tools
scissors

Materials
thin card

Instructions

1. Cut out the whizzer shape.

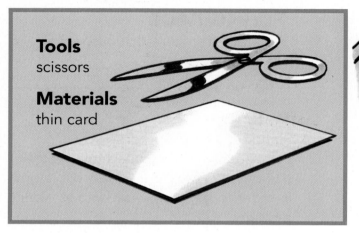

2. Cut out the whizzer whip shape.

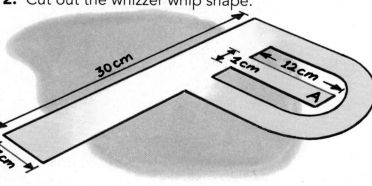

Flying instructions

1. To fly the whizzer, insert the end of whip at A under the whizzer rim, over the whizzer hub and under the far rim.

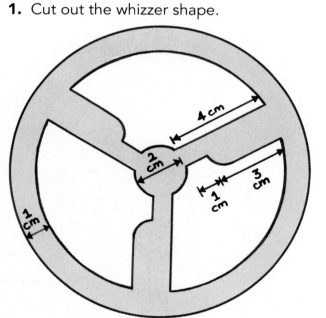

Then give the whizzer a forehand flick of the wrist.

FLYING FACT
The first helicopter flight was made by Paul Cornu in 1907. In a machine made of bicycle parts, Monsieur Cornu was airborne for twenty seconds at a height of 30cm!

Make a Helicopter Spinner

Your whizzer shows how easily helicopter blades can cut through the air. The second part of this challenge is to make helicopter blades which go round and round.

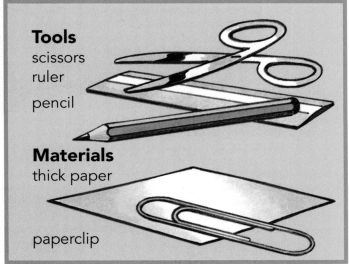

Tools
scissors
ruler
pencil

Materials
thick paper

paperclip

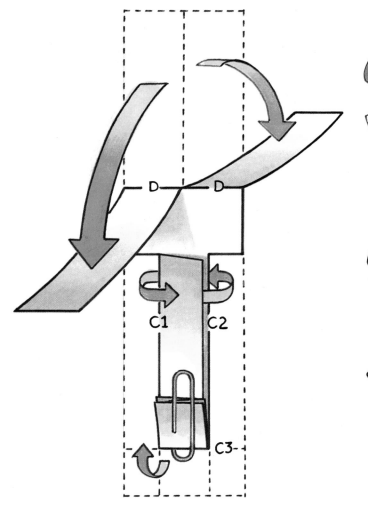

Instructions

1. Draw the lines as shown and cut along lines A and B.

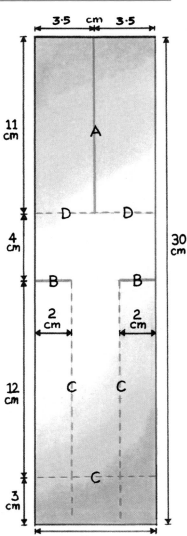

3·5 cm 3·5

11 cm — A

D — D

4 cm

B — B

2 cm   2 cm

12 cm   C — C

30 cm

3 cm   C

7 cm

2. Fold the paper at C and D as shown. Attach the paperclip as shown.

3. Drop your helicopter spinner from a height indoors. Try several drops - do the blades always spin the same way?

Make a 'Jet' Plane

Until the 1930s all planes were propeller driven. Jet engines allowed planes to travel faster. In a turbojet, air is drawn into the engine and compressed by a turbine. The compressed air is then mixed with fuel in the combustion chamber and ignited. Hot gases shoot out of the rear nozzle pushing the plane forward and powering the compressor turbine.

For this challenge you have to make your own jet powered plane using the compressed air power of a balloon.

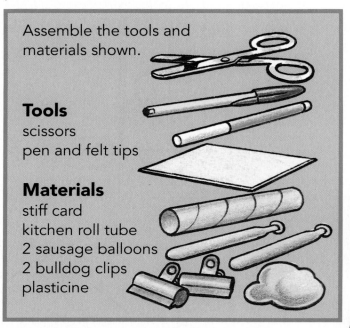

Assemble the tools and materials shown.

Tools
scissors
pen and felt tips

Materials
stiff card
kitchen roll tube
2 sausage balloons
2 bulldog clips
plasticine

2. Make slots in the side of the kitchen roll tube for the wing. Make slots as shown from the tail pieces. Decorate the tube with felt tips.

3. Slot the wing and tail pieces through the roll. Secure with parcel tape. Bend the wings as shown.

Instructions
1. Cut the wing shape and tail shapes from card.

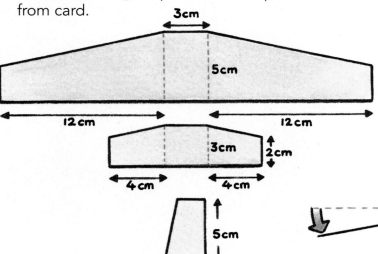

3cm

5cm

12 cm   12 cm

3cm   2cm

4 cm   4 cm

5cm

3cm

Look at the plane from the front and check that the wings and tail are level on either side.

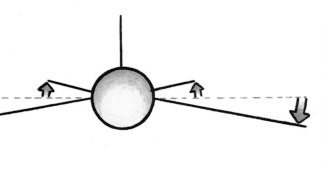

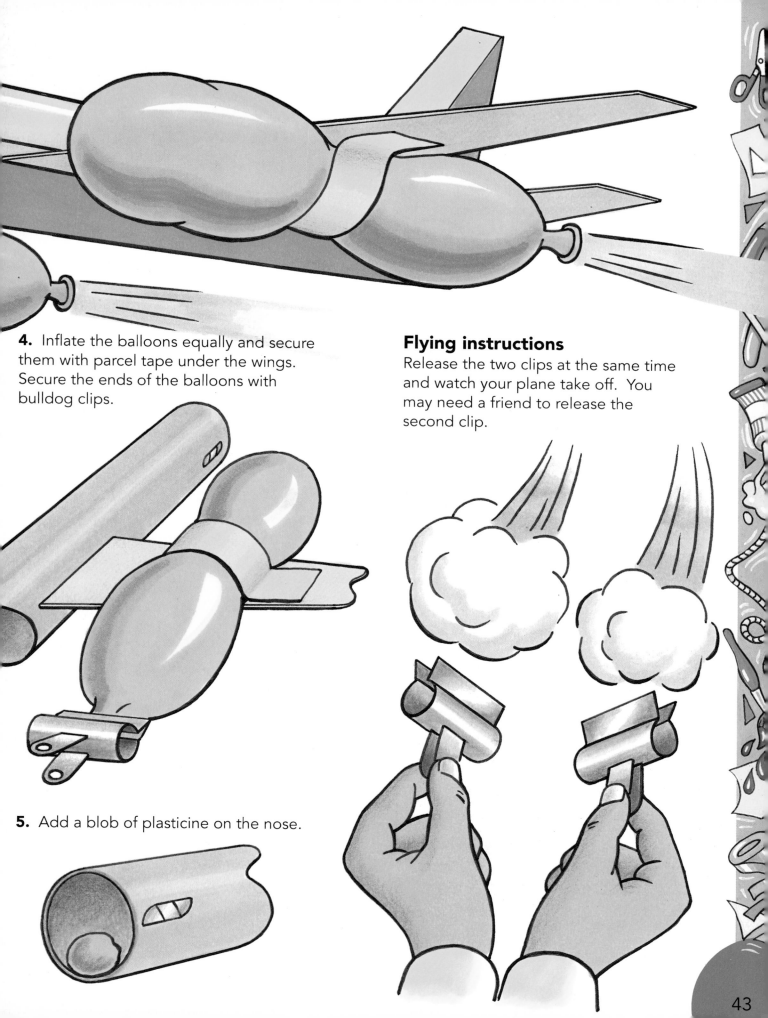

4. Inflate the balloons equally and secure them with parcel tape under the wings. Secure the ends of the balloons with bulldog clips.

5. Add a blob of plasticine on the nose.

Flying instructions

Release the two clips at the same time and watch your plane take off. You may need a friend to release the second clip.

The Final Frontier

Planes cannot fly in space. Propellers need to push against air and jet engines need air to work. In space there is no air, so a different kind of flying machine is required. Rockets carry their own fuel and oxygen supply in liquid form. The fuel and oxygen is mixed and ignited and the hot gases blasting from the back nozzle thrust the rocket upwards.

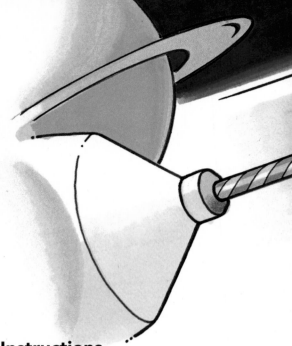

For this challenge you have to make a rocket. But it doesn't have to go into orbit!

Assemble the tools and materials shown.

Tools
ruler
scissors

Materials
washing-up liquid bottle
2 plastic straws, one narrower than the other
modelling clay or plasticine
parcel tape
thin card

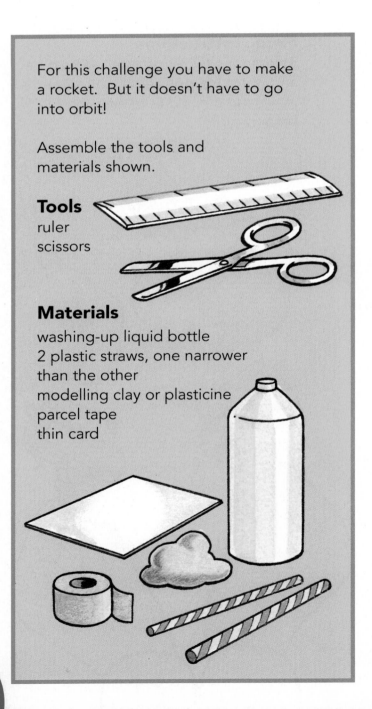

Instructions
1. Make a hole in the top of the washing-up liquid bottle and push the narrower straw through. Seal the gap where the straw emerges from the bottle with plasticine and parcel tape.

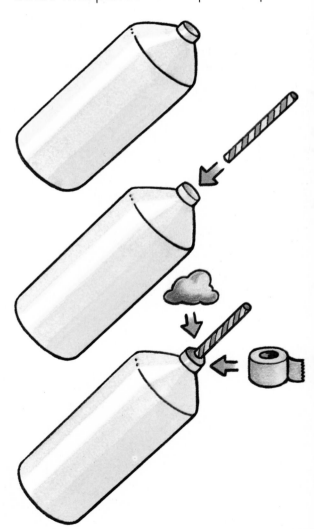

2. To make the rocket, cut about 10cm off the length of the larger straw. Make tail fins as shown and stick them to the straw with sticky tape.

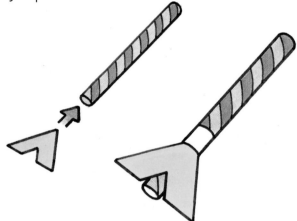

3. Make a nose cone from plasticine.

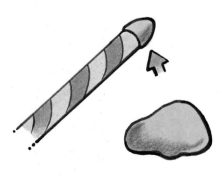

Flying instructions
Slide the rocket straw over the launch straw. Squeeze the bottle firmly and watch the rocket take off.

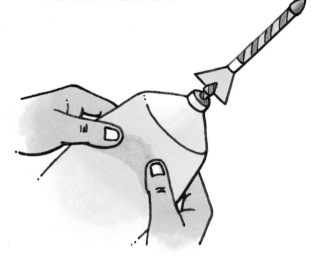

How it works
When you squeeze the bottle the air inside is compressed. The air is forced into the rocket and pushes it into the air.

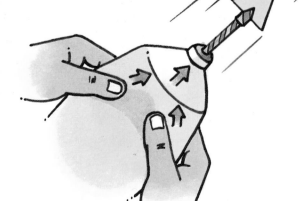

Plane Sailing

Passenger aeroplane services began in 1919. At that time there was a shortage of runways in many parts of the world. One answer was to develop planes which could land on the sea. Seaplanes have boat shaped bodies and wing pontoons to stabilise the plane as it lands in the waves.

Can you make a model seaplane?

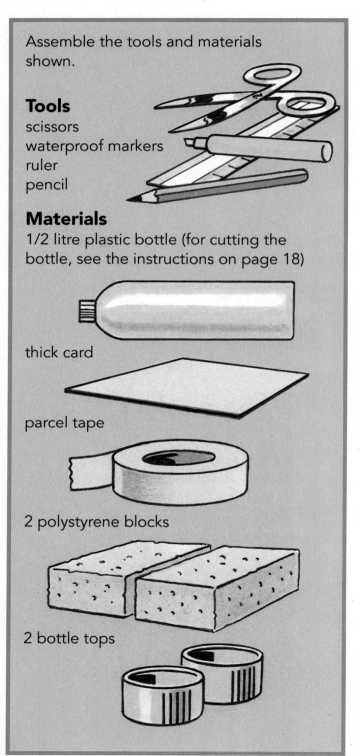

Assemble the tools and materials shown.

Tools
scissors
waterproof markers
ruler
pencil

Materials
1/2 litre plastic bottle (for cutting the bottle, see the instructions on page 18)

thick card

parcel tape

2 polystyrene blocks

2 bottle tops

Instructions
1. Ask an adult to help you make slots in the bottle as shown.

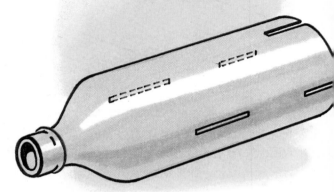

2. Cut out the wing and tail pieces and pontoon supports on thick card to sizes shown.

X = WIDTH OF BASE OF BOTTLE

X   X   X

WING

TAILPLANE

3 cm   X   3 cm

FIN

X
+
2·5
cm

X

3 cm
3 cm
3 cm

A   A
A   A

PONTOON SUPPORT

3. Slot the wing and tail pieces into the bottle slots. Secure the slots with parcel tape to make sure that the bottle will not leak.

Decoration
Add details such as identification markings, logos, and the cabin using waterproof markers.

4. Fold the pontoon supports along line A and stick them under the wings with parcel tape. Use more parcel tape to attach the other ends of the supports to the polystyrene blocks.

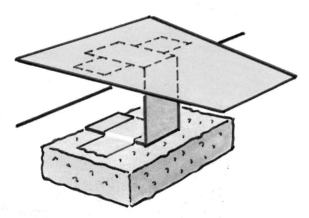

5. Tape the bottle tops to the wings to make the engines.

Testing
Your seaplane is not intended to fly, but it should float. Turn the page to discover how to make it star in an action drama.

A Real Life Drama

The final challenge is the most difficult of all because you have to invent it yourself! To begin with, you need to consider the following:

Setting

You could make a good setting using an old blue sheet or blanket thrown over some furniture. This could be the sea or sky. You could make an interesting lighting effect by placing an unshaded light or torch behind the sheet (do not place the lamp close to the sheet).

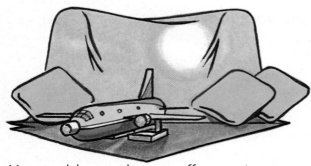

You could record some effects using a tape recorder.

Write a Script

To write the drama you need to find out a little more about seaplanes and how they are used around the world.

A seaplane will normally land near a jetty or pick-up ship. Seaplanes cannot land in rough seas but they can land near the shore and roll up a beach. These facts could provide material for an air sea rescue drama. Before you start, make some notes about your characters, their personalities and how they might react to one another in the drama.